EXPRESSIONS OF LOVE

A TREASURY OF LOVE POEMS AND LOVE QUOTES

JOHN SCAGLIONE

A Treasury of Love Poems
and Love Quotes

Expressions of Love

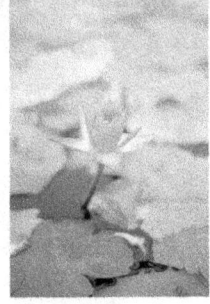

John Scaglione

Copyrights © 2020 by John Scaglione All rights reserved

including the right of reproduction

in whole or in part in any form.

Published by Green House Books

Reproduction or translations of any part of this book beyond what is permissible by Sections 107 or 108 of the 1976 United States Copyright Act without express written permission from the copyright owner is unlawful.

ISBN: 978-0-9826263-1-3 (Ebook)

ISBN-13: 978-0-9826263-2-0

Great acknowledgement is made to the authors of the poems and quotes whose works are in the public domain which made this project possible.

To my lovely wife Christi. Thank you for sharing this Funtastic adventure called life. You inspire and encourage me to greatness.

To my children Danica & Tyler who are love made visible and help me love everyday

To my parents Colleen & Frank for creating a life worth living inspiring me to be loving, kind and thoughtful to everyone.

Expressions of Love

A Treasury of Love Poems and Quotes

John Scaglione

I am truly appreciative and thankful for you taking time out of your busy life to acknowledge my work. It is my sincere hope, each piece in this publication will kindle the fire of love in your hearts that will last forever.

CONTENTS

PART I

I believe in Love	3
How Do I Love Thee? (Sonnet 43)	5
I Love Her	6
If All Else Perished	7
To See Her	8
Longing	9
Be Thou the Rainbow	11
Song of Secret Love	12
I Think of Love and You	14
Hold Down a Rainbow	15
Stole My Heart Away Complete	16
Beyond Her Smile	17
The CLOD and the PEBBLE	18
Cloudless Heaven	19
Because She Would Ask Me Why I Loved Her	20
Two Souls	22
First Love	23
Your Words in the Dark	25
Your Words Are My Food	26
Love	27
My Heart is Like a Singing Bird	28
When You Look at Me	29
A Valentine to My Wife	30
Tread Softly	32
Sweetheart Fair	33
There Is a Lady Sweet and Kind	34
My Very Greatest Happiness	35
I love You More	36
Beautiful Dreamer	37
My Love for You is a Journey	39
True Love	40
My Heart Will Never Forget You	41

My Love's a Match	42
To A Stranger	44
I Only Need You	46
The Indian Serenade	47
Vast Is My Love	49
The Rose of Sharon	50
Love's Philosophy	52
The Welcome	54
Wondrous Moment	56
To Anthea	58
The Passionate Shepherd to His Love	59

PART II
LOVE QUOTES

If I Had a Flower	63
Romance	64
One Word	65
A Song Only You Can Hear	66
We Loved with a Love	67
Love Looks	68
In Vain I Have Struggled	69
The Real Lover	70
Love Is Eternal	71
What Ever Our Souls are Made of	72
Your Footfall	73
Driven by the Force of Love	74
Love is the Master Key	75
Thou Art Fairer	76
You and You Alone	77
Every Heart Sings	78
Absence	79
Distance	80
Find Someone	81
Once in a While	82
Someday	83
To Love a Person	84
One Day	85
We Are Afraid	86
The Beauty of the Soul	87
Rejoice	88

You and Me in One	89
That Which is Loved	90
The Greatest Gift	91
The Heart Has Reasons	92
Tenderness	93
One Happiness	94
No Remedy for Love	95
Till I Loved	96
To Love for the Sake of Loving	97
To Love Someone	98
To the World	99
True Poets	100
Who So Loves	101
I Miss You so Much	102
You Are Everything To Me	103

PART I

I BELIEVE IN LOVE
BY JOHN SCAGLIONE

∼

Every smile you bestow upon me,
every kiss that enchants my lips, your
whispers in my ear excite me
and you touch my soul with wit.
Soul to soul,
deep to deep calls my love for you.
In thee I'll delight forever for
I believe in Love

Like a fire fly magically lights up the night, even for just a fleeting
moment
I believe in Love

As a gazelle leaps though the air with excitement, anticipation
and joy,
I believe in Love

I boldly confess to the world my love for you

no matter the consequence,
I believe in Love

When stars fall to make wishes come true,
I believe in Love

To love for loves sake and no thing else,
I believe in Love

My love for you is like an uncontrollable volcano, a force of nature,
majestically erupting and all consuming
I believe in Love

HOW DO I LOVE THEE? (SONNET 43)
ELIZABETH BARRETT BROWNING, 1806 - 1861

How do I love thee? Let me count the ways.
I love thee to the depth and breadth and height
My soul can reach, when feeling out of sight
For the ends of being and ideal grace.
I love thee to the level of every day's
Most quiet need, by sun and candle-light.
I love thee freely, as men strive for right.
I love thee purely, as they turn from praise.
I love thee with the passion put to use
In my old griefs, and with my childhood's faith.
I love thee with a love I seemed to lose
With my lost saints. I love thee with the breath,
Smiles, tears, of all my life; and, if God choose,
I shall but love thee better after death.

I LOVE HER

F. SCOTT FITZGERALD 1896 - 1940 (POEM WRITTEN FOR HIS WIFE ZELDA)

∼

"I fell in love with her courage, her sincerity, and her flaming self respect. And it's these things I'd believe in, even if the whole world indulged in wild suspicions that she wasn't all she should be. I love her and it is the beginning of everything."

∼

IF ALL ELSE PERISHED

, 1818 -1847 WUTHERING HEIGHTS

"If all else perished and he remained,
I should still continue to be;
and if all else remained, and he were annihilated,
the universe would turn to a mighty stranger."

TO SEE HER

ROBERT BURNS 1759 - 1796

∽

But to see her, was to love her,
love but her, and her alone.

∽

LONGING

MATTHEW ARNOLD 1822 1888

Come to me in my dreams, and then
By day I shall be well again.
For then the night will more than pay
The hopeless longing of the day.

Come, as thou cam'st a thousand times,
A messenger from radiant climes,
And smile on thy new world, and be
As kind to others as to me.

Or, as thou never cam'st in sooth,
Come now, and let me dream it truth.
And part my hair, and kiss my brow,
And say My love! why sufferest thou?

Come to me in my dreams, and then
By day I shall be well again.
For then the night will more than pay
The hopeless longing of the day.

BE THOU THE RAINBOW

LORD BYRON 1788-1824

∼

Be thou the rainbow in the storms of life.
The evening beam that smiles the clouds away
and tints tomorrow with prophetic ray.

∼

SONG OF SECRET LOVE

JOHN CLARE 1793-1864

∼

I hid my love when young while I
Couldn't bear the buzzing of a fly
I hid my love to my despite
Till I could not bear to look at light
I dare not gaze upon her face
But left her memory in each place
Where ere I saw a wild flower lie
I kissed and bade my love goodbye

I met her in the greenest dells
Where dew drops pearl the wood bluebells
The lost breeze kissed her bright blue eye
The bee kissed and went singing by
A sunbeam found a passage there
A gold chain round her neck so fair
As secret as the wild bee's song
She lay there all the summer long

I hid my love in field and town
Till e'en the breeze would knock me down
The bees seemed singing ballads l'er
The fly's buss turned a Lion's roar
And even silence found a tongue
To haunt me all the summer long
The riddle nature could not prove
Was nothing else but secret love

I THINK OF LOVE AND YOU
EMILY DICKINSON 1830-1886

∼

I think of love and you and my heart grows
full and warm,
and my breath stands still. I can feel a sunshine stealing into my soul
and making it all summer,
and every thorn, a rose.

∼

HOLD DOWN A RAINBOW
AUTHOR UNKNOWN

I wish I could hold down the rainbow,
write your name on it and place it back,
so that the world can see how colorful
life is to have you as my love

STOLE MY HEART AWAY COMPLETE
JOHN CLARE 1793-1864

∼

I ne'er was struck before that hour
with love so sudden and so sweet.
Her face it bloomed like a sweet flower
and stole my heart away complete

∼

BEYOND HER SMILE
ANDRE GIDE 1869-1951

I wished for nothing beyond her smile,
and to walk with her thus,
hand in hand, along a sun warmed,
flower bordered path.

THE CLOD AND THE PEBBLE

WILLIAM BLAKE 1757-1827

∼

Love seeketh not Itself to please,
Nor for itself hath any care;
But for another gives its ease,
And builds a Heaven in Hells despair.

So sang a little Clod of Clay,
Trodden with the cattle's feet;
But a Pebble of the brook,
Warbled out these metres meet.

Love seeketh only Self to please,

To bind another to Its delight:
Joys in anothers loss of ease,
And builds a Hell in Heavens despite.

∼

CLOUDLESS HEAVEN

VICTOR HUGO 1802-1885

What I feel for you seems less of earth
and more of cloudless heaven.

~

BECAUSE SHE WOULD ASK ME WHY I LOVED HER

CHRISTOPHER BRENNAN 1870-1932

~

If questioning would make us wise
No eyes would ever gaze in eyes;
If all our tale were told in speech
No mouths would wander each to each.

Were spirits free from mortal mesh
And love not bound in hearts of flesh
No aching breasts would yearn to meet
And find their ecstasy complete.

For who is there that lives and knows
The secret powers by which he grows?
Were knowledge all, what were our need
To thrill and faint and sweetly bleed?

Then seek not, sweet, the "If" and "Why"
I love you now until I die.
For I must love because I live
And life in me is what you give.

TWO SOULS
JOHN KEATS 1795-1821

∼

Two souls with but a single thought,
two hearts that beat as one.

∼

FIRST LOVE

JOHN CLARE 1793-1864

I ne'er was struck before that hour
With love so sudden and so sweet.
Her face it bloomed like a sweet flower
And stole my heart away complete.

My face turned pale, a deadly pale.
My legs refused to walk away,
And when she looked what could I ail
My life and all seemed turned to clay.

And then my blood rushed to my face
And took my eyesight quite away.
The trees and bushes round the place
Seemed midnight at noonday.

I could not see a single thing,
Words from my eyes did start.
They spoke as chords do from the string,

And blood burnt round my heart.

Are flowers the winter's choice
Is love's bed always snow
She seemed to hear my silent voice
Not love appeals to know.

I never saw so sweet a face
As that I stood before.
My heart has left its dwelling place
And can return no more.

YOUR WORDS IN THE DARK

AMY LOWELL 1874-1925

Brighter than fireflies upon the Uji River
are your words in the dark, Beloved.

~

YOUR WORDS ARE MY FOOD
BEN JONSON 1572-1637

∼

Your words are my food
Drink to me only with thine eyes,
and I will pledge with mine;
Or leave a kiss but in the cup
and I'll not look for wine.

∼

LOVE
SAMUEL TAYLOR COLERIDGE 1772-1834

∼

And in life's noisiest hour,
There whispers still the ceaseless love of thee,
The heart's self-solace and soliloquy.
You mould my hopes, you fashion me within ;
And to the leading love-throb in the heart
Thro' all my being, thro' my pulse's beat ;
You lie in all my many thoughts, like light,
Like the fair light of dawn, or summer eve
On rippling stream, or cloud-reflecting lake.
And looking to the heaven,
that bends above you,
How oft! I bless the lot that made me love you.

∼

MY HEART IS LIKE A SINGING BIRD
CHRISTINA ROSSETTI 1830-1894

My heart is like a singing bird
whose nest is a watered shoot;
My heart is like an apple tree
whose boughs are bent with thickest fruit;
My heart is like a rainbow shell
that paddles in a halcyon sea;
My heart is gladder than all these
because my love is come to me.

WHEN YOU LOOK AT ME
WILLIAM MAKEPEACE THACKERAY 1811-1863

When you look at me, when you think of me,
I am in paradise.

~

A VALENTINE TO MY WIFE

EUGENE FIELD 1850-1895

∽

Accept, dear girl, this little token,
And if between the lines you seek,
You'll find the love I've often spoken
The love my dying lips shall speak.

Our little ones are making merry
O'er am'rous ditties rhymed in jest,
But in these words (though awkward very)
The genuine article's expressed.

You are as fair and sweet and tender,
Dear brown-eyed little sweetheart mine,
As when, a callow youth and slender,
I asked to be your Valentine.

What though these years of ours be fleeting?
What though the years of youth be flown?
I'll mock old Tempus with repeating,

"I love my love and her alone!"

And when I fall before his reaping,
And when my stuttering speech is dumb,
Think not my love is dead or sleeping,
But that it waits for you to come.

So take, dear love, this little token,
And if there speaks in any line
The sentiment I'd fain have spoken, Say, will you kiss your Valentine?

TREAD SOFTLY
WILLIAM YEATS 1865-1939

~

I have spread my dreams under your feet.
Tread softly because you tread on my dreams.

~

SWEETHEART FAIR

MINNA THOMAS ANTRIM 1861-1950

∼

Brew me a cup for a winter's night.
For the wind howls loud and the furies fight;
Spice it with love and stir it with care,
And I'll toast your bright eyes, my sweetheart fair.

∼

THERE IS A LADY SWEET AND KIND

THOMAS FORD 1580 - 1648

∽

There is a lady sweet and kind,
Was never a face so pleased my mind;
I did but see her passing by,
And yet I'll love her till I die.

Her gesture, motion, and her smiles,
Her wit, her voice my heart beguiles,
Beguiles my heart, I know not why,
And yet I'll love her till I die.

Cupid is winged and he doth range,
Her country, so, my love doth change:
But change she earth, or change she sky,
Yet, I will love her till I die.

∽

MY VERY GREATEST HAPPINESS
AUTHOR UNKNOWN

∼

Because I love you truly,
Because you love me, too,
My very greatest happiness
Is sharing life with you.

∼

I LOVE YOU MORE

ROSEMONDE GÉRARD 1871–1953 (FROM THE POEM ETERNAL SONG)

∼

Each day I love you more,
Today more than yesterday
and less than tomorrow

∼

BEAUTIFUL DREAMER

STEPHEN FOSTER 1826-1864

∽

Beautiful dreamer, wake unto me,
Starlight and dewdrops are waiting for thee;
Sounds of the rude world heard in the day,
Lull'd by the moonlight have all pass'd a way.

Beautiful dreamer, queen of my song,
List while I woo thee with soft melody;
Gone are the cares of life's busy throng,
Beautiful dreamer, awake unto me.

Beautiful dreamer, out on the sea
Mermaids are chaunting the wild lorelie;
Over the streamlet vapors are borne,
Waiting to fade at the bright coming morn.

Beautiful dreamer, beam on my heart,
E'en as the morn on the streamlet and sea;
Then will all clouds of sorrow depart,
Beautiful dreamer, awake unto me.

MY LOVE FOR YOU IS A JOURNEY
AUTHOR UNKNOWN

∼

My love for you is a journey...
Starting at forever...
And ending at never.

∼

TRUE LOVE
AUTHOR UNKNOWN

∽

True love is a sacred flame
that burns eternally.
And none can dim its special glow
or change its destiny.
True love speaks in tender tones
and hears with gentle ear,
True love gives with open heart
and true love conquers fear.
True love makes no harsh demands
it neither rules nor binds,
And true love holds with gentle hands
the hearts that it entwines.

∽

MY HEART WILL NEVER FORGET YOU

AUTHOR UNKNOWN

If the days won't allow us to see each other,
memories will,
and if my eyes can't see you,
my heart will never forget you.

MY LOVE'S A MATCH
ALFRED P. GRAVES 1846-1931

∼

My Love's a match in beauty
For every flower that blows,
Her little ear's a lilly,
Her velvet cheek a rose;
Her locks are gilly gowans
Hang golden to her knee.
If I were King of Ireland,
My Queen she'd surely be.

Her eyes are fond forget-me-nots,
And no such snow is seen
Upon the heaving hawthorn bush
As crests her bodice green.
The thrushes when she's talking
Sit listening on the tree.

If I were King of Ireland,
My Queen she'd surely be.

TO A STRANGER

WALT WHITMAN 1819–1892 LEAVES OF GRASS

∼

Passing stranger! you do not know
How longingly I look upon you,
You must be he I was seeking,
Or she I was seeking (It comes to me as a dream)

I have somewhere surely
Lived a life of joy with you,
All is recall'd as we flit by each other,
Fluid, affectionate, chaste, matured,

You grew up with me,
Were a boy with me or a girl with me,
I ate with you and slept with you, your body has become
not yours only nor left my body mine only,

You give me the pleasure of your eyes,
face, flesh as we pass,
You take of my beard, breast, hands,
in return,

I am not to speak to you, I am to think of you
when I sit alone or wake at night, alone
I am to wait, I do not doubt I am to meet you again
I am to see to it that I do not lose you.

I ONLY NEED YOU
AUTHOR UNKNOWN

∼

I need many things to help me live
but I need only you
to make life worth living.

∼

THE INDIAN SERENADE
PERCY BYSSHE SHELLEY 1731-1815

I arise from dreams of thee
In the first sweet sleep or night,
When the winds are breathing low,
And the stars are shining bright.
I arise from dreams of thee,
And a spirit in my feet
Has led me-who knows how? –
To thy chamber-window, sweet!

The wandering airs they faint
On the dark, the silent stream,-
The champak odors fail
Like sweet thoughts in a dream;
The nightingale's complaint,
It dies upon her heart,
As I must die on thine,

O, beloved as thou art!

O, lift me from the grass!
I die, I faint, I fail!
Let thy love in kisses rain
On my lips and eyelids pale.
My cheek is cold and white, alas!
My heart beats loud and fast:
Oh! press it close to thine again,
Where it will break at last!

∼

VAST IS MY LOVE
AUTHOR UNKNOWN

My love for you is so vast
I could never keep it a secret,
Vast is my love for you
a secret I could never keep quiet.

THE ROSE OF SHARON

SONG OF SOLOMON 2:1-8

∽

I am the rose of Sharon,
and the lily of the valleys.
As the lily among thorns,
so is my love among the daughters.
As the apple tree among the trees of the wood,
so is my beloved among the sons.

I sat down under his shadow with great delight,
and his fruit was sweet to my taste.
He brought me to the banqueting house,
and his banner over me was love.
Stay me with flagons, comfort me with apples:
for I am sick of love.

His left hand is under my head,
and his right hand doth embrace me.
I charge you, O ye daughters of Jerusalem,
by the roes, and by the hinds of the field...
that ye stir not up, nor awake my love...
till he please.

The voice of my beloved! behold, he cometh
leaping upon the mountains, skipping upon the hills.

LOVE'S PHILOSOPHY

PERCY BYSSHE SHELLEY 1731-1815

The fountains mingle with the river,
And the rivers with the ocean;
The winds of heaven mix forever,
With a sweet emotion;
Nothing in the world is single;
All things by a law divine
In one another's being mingle;–
Why not I with thine?

See! the mountains kiss high heaven,
And the waves clasp one another;
No sister flower would be forgiven,
If it disdained it's brother;
And the sunlight clasps the earth,
And the moonbeams kiss the sea;–

What are all these kissings worth,
    If thou kiss not me?

THE WELCOME

THOMAS OSBORNE DAVIS (1814–45)

~

COME in the evening, or come in the morning;
Come when you 're look'd for, or come without warning:
Kisses and welcome you 'll find here before you,
And the oftener you come here the more I 'll adore you!
Light is my heart since the day we were plighted;
Red is my cheek that they told me was blighted;
The green of the trees looks far greener than ever,
And the linnets are singing, "True lovers don't sever!"

I 'll pull you sweet flowers, to wear if you choose them,
Or, after you've kiss'd them, they 'll lie on my bosom;
I 'll fetch from the mountain its breeze to inspire you;
I 'll fetch from my fancy a tale that won't tire you.
Oh! your step's like the rain to the summer-vex'd farmer,
Or sabre and shield to a knight without armor;
I 'll sing you sweet songs till the stars rise above me,
Then, wandering, I 'll wish you in silence to love me.
We 'll look through the trees at the cliff and the eyrie;

We 'll tread round the rath on the track of the fairy;
We 'll look on the stars, and we 'll list to the river,
Till you ask of your darling what gift you can give her:
Oh! she 'll whisper you—"Love, as unchangeably beaming,
And trust, when in secret, most tunefully streaming;
Till the starlight of heaven above us shall quiver,
As our souls flow in one down eternity's river."
So come in the evening, or come in the morning;
Come when you 're looked for, or come without warning:
Kisses and welcome you 'll find here before you,
And the oftener you come here the more I 'll adore you!
Light is my heart since the day we were plighted
Red is my cheek that they told me was blighted;
The green of the trees looks far greener than ever,
And the linnets are singing, "True lovers don't sever!"

WONDROUS MOMENT
ALEXANDER PUSHKIN 1799-1837

∼

The wondrous moment of our meeting . . .
I well remember you appear
Before me like a vision fleeting,
A beauty's angel pure and clear.

In hopeless ennui surrounding
The worldly bustle, to my ear
For long your tender voice kept sounding,
For long in dreams came features dear.

Time passed. Unruly storms confounded
Old dreams, and I from year to year
Forgot how tender you had sounded,
Your heavenly features once so dear.

My backwoods days dragged slow and quiet —
Dull fence around, dark vault above —
Devoid of God and uninspired,
Devoid of tears, of fire, of love.

Sleep from my soul began retreating,
And here you once again appear
Before me like a vision fleeting,
A beauty's angel pure and clear.

In ecstasy the heart is beating,
Old joys for it anew revive;
Inspired and God-filled, it is greeting
The fire, and tears, and love alive.

TO ANTHEA

ROBERT HERRICK 1591-1674

AH, my Anthea! Must my heart still break?
(Love makes me write, what shame forbids to speak)
Give me a kiss, and to that kiss a score;
Then to that twenty add a hundred more:
A thousand to that hundred: so kiss on,
To make that thousand up a million.
Treble that million, and when that is done
Let's kiss afresh, as when we first begun.
But yet, though love likes well such scenes as these,
There is an act that will more fully please:
Kissing and glancing, soothing, all make way
But to the acting of this private play:
Name it I would; but, being blushing red,
The rest I'll speak when we meet both in bed.

THE PASSIONATE SHEPHERD TO HIS LOVE

CHRISTOPHER MARLOWE 1564-1593

Come live with me and be my love,
And we will all the pleasures prove,
That valleys, groves, hills and fields,
Woods or steepy mountains yields.

And we will sit upon the rocks,
Seeing the shepherds feed their flocks
By shallow rivers, to whose falls
Melodious birds sing madrigals.

And I will make thee beds of roses,
And a thousand fragrant posies,
A cap of flowers and a kirtle
Embroidered all with leaves of myrtle;

A gown made of the finest wool,
Which from our pretty lambs we pull;
Fair-lined slippers for the cold,
With buckles of the purest gold;

A belt of straw and ivy buds,
With coral clasps and amber studs;
And if these pleasures may thee move,
Come live with me and be my love.

The shepherd swains shall dance and sing
For thy delight each May morning;
If these delights thy mind may move,
Then live with me and be my love.

∼

PART II
LOVE QUOTES

IF I HAD A FLOWER

LORD ALFRED TENNYSON 1809 - 1892

"If I had a flower for every time I thought of you
I could walk through my garden forever."

ROMANCE
ELINOR GLEN 1864 - 1943

∼

"Romance is the glamour which turns the dust
of everyday life into a golden haze."

∼

ONE WORD

SOPHOCLES 496BC - 405BC

"One word Frees us of all the weight and pain of life:
That word is love."

A SONG ONLY YOU CAN HEAR

OSCAR WILDE 1854 - 1900

∽

"You don't love someone for their looks,
or their clothes or for their fancy
car, but because they
sing a song only you can hear."

∽

WE LOVED WITH A LOVE
EDGAR ALLAN POE 1809 - 1949

"We loved with a love
that was more than love."

LOVE LOOKS

WILLIAM SHAKESPEARE 1564 -1616

∼

"Love looks not with the eyes,
but with the mind,
And therefore is winged Cupid painted blind."

∼

IN VAIN I HAVE STRUGGLED

JANE AUSTEN 1775-1817

∼

"In vain have I struggled. It will not do.
My feelings will not be repressed.
You must allow me to tell you how ardently
I admire and love you."

∼

THE REAL LOVER

MARILYN MONROE - (NORMA JEANE MORTENSON) 1926 - 1962

"The real lover is the man who can thrill you by kissing your forehead or smiling into your eyes or just staring into space."

LOVE IS ETERNAL

E.M. FORSTER 1879 - 1970

"It isn't possible to love and part.
You will wish that it was.
You can transmute love, ignore it, muddle it,
but you can never pull it out of you.
I know by experience that the poets are right: love is eternal."

WHAT EVER OUR SOULS ARE MADE OF

EMILY BRONTE 1818-1848

∽

Whatever our souls are made of...
his and mine are the same

∽

YOUR FOOTFALL
CONSTANTINE CAVAFY 1863-1933

∾

My life has been awaiting you.
Your footfall was my own heart's beat.

∾

DRIVEN BY THE FORCE OF LOVE
PIERRE TEILHARD DE CHARDIN 1881-1955

∼

Driven by the force of love the fragments
of the world
seek each other that the world may come
into being.

∼

LOVE IS THE MASTER KEY

OLIVER WENDELL HOLMES 1809-1894

Love is not a matter of counting the years,
it is making the years count.
Love is the master key that opens
the gates of happiness.

~

THOU ART FAIRER
CHRISTOPHER MARLOWE 1564-1593

∼

Thou are fairer than the evening air
clad in the beauty of a thousand stars.

∼

YOU AND YOU ALONE

GEORGE MOORE 1852-1933

∼

You, and you alone,
make me feel that I am alive.
Other men, it is said, have seen angels.
But I have seen thee, and thou art enough.

∼

EVERY HEART SINGS

PLATO 429BC - 347BC

∼

Every heart sings a song incomplete,
until another heart whispers back.
Those who wish to sing always find a song.
At the touch of a lover, everyone becomes a poet.

∼

ABSENCE

FRANCOIS DE LA ROCHEFOUCAULD 1613-1680

∿

Absence diminishes commonplace passions
and increases great ones.
As the wind extinguishes candles and kindles fires.

∿

DISTANCE
AUTHOR UNKNOWN

∼

Distance means so little
when someone means so much.

∼

FIND SOMEONE
AUTHOR UNKNOWN

Everyone comes with baggage.
Find someone who loves you
enough to help you unpack.

ONCE IN A WHILE
AUTHOR UNKNOWN

∼

Once in a while,
right in the middle of an ordinary life,
love gives us a fairy tale.

∼

SOMEDAY
AUTHOR UNKNOWN

∼

Someday, someone will walk into your life
and make you realize why
it never worked out with anyone else.

∼

TO LOVE A PERSON

ARNE GARBORG 1851 - 1924

∼

To love a person is to learn the
song that is in their heart,
and to sing it to them
when they have forgotten.

∼

ONE DAY

AUTHOR UNKNOWN

One day someone is going to hug you so tight
that all of your broken pieces
will stick back together

WE ARE AFRAID

ELEANOR ROOSEVELT 1884-1962

∽

We are afraid to care too much,
for fear that the other person does
not care at all.

∽

THE BEAUTY OF THE SOUL

SAINT AUGUSTINE 354-430

∼

"Since love grows within you so beauty grows.
For love is the beauty of the soul."

∼

REJOICE

CARL EWALD 1856-1908

∾

Take Spring when it comes and rejoice.
Take happiness when it comes and rejoice.
Take love when it comes and rejoice.

∾

YOU AND ME IN ONE
CHARLOTTE BRONTË, JANE EYRE

I have for the first time found
what I can truly love. I have found you.
You are my sympathy, my better self,
my good angel. I am bound to you
with a strong attachment. I think you good, gifted, lovely: a fervent,
a solemn passion is conceived in my heart;
it leans to you, draws you to my
centre and spring of life, wrap my existence about you–and,
kindling in
pure, powerful flame, fuses you and me in one

THAT WHICH IS LOVED
NORWEGIAN PROVERB

That which is loved is always beautiful

~

THE GREATEST GIFT
AUTHOR UNKNOWN

The greatest gift I could ever give you would be
to see yourself through my eyes

THE HEART HAS REASONS

BLAISE PASCAL 1623-1662

∽

The heart has reasons
that reason does not understand

∽

TENDERNESS
VICTOR HUGO 1802-1885

The most powerful symptom of love
is a tenderness which becomes
at times almost insupportable

~

ONE HAPPINESS
GEORGE SAND 1804-1876

∽

There is only one happiness in life:
to love and be loved

∽

NO REMEDY FOR LOVE

HENRY DAVID THOREAU

∼

There is no remedy for love but to love more

∼

TILL I LOVED
EMILY DICKINSON 1830-1886

Till I loved I never lived

~

TO LOVE FOR THE SAKE OF LOVING
ALPHONSE MARIE LOUIS DE PRAT DE LAMARTINE (1790-1869)

To love for the sake of being loved is human,
but to love for the sake of loving is angelic

TO LOVE SOMEONE
FRANCOIS MAURIAC 1885-1970

∿

To love someone
is to see a miracle invisible to others

∿

TO THE WORLD
AUTHOR UNKNOWN

To the world you may be one person,
but to one person
you may be their world

TRUE POETS
AUTHOR UNKNOWN

∼

True poets don't write their
thoughts with a pen...
They release the ink that flows
from within their heart."

∼

WHO SO LOVES
ELIZABETH BARRETT BROWNING 1806-1861

Who so loves
believes the impossible

I MISS YOU SO MUCH
AUTHOR UNKNOWN

∼

I miss you so much that
you're always on my mind.
I love you so much that
you're always in my heart

∼

YOU ARE EVERYTHING TO ME

SARAH BERNHARDT 1844 -1923

∼

Your words are my food
Your breath my wine
You are everything to me

∼

www.ingramcontent.com/pod-product-compliance
Lightning Source LLC
Chambersburg PA
CBHW031452040426
42444CB00007B/1067